FAILING FORWARD

Also by Alan Migliorato:

The Manly Art of Raising a Daughter

FAILING FORWARD

LEADERSHIP LESSONS FOR CATHOLIC TEENS TODAY

ALAN MIGLIORATO & DARRYL DZIEDZIC

SOPHIA INSTITUTE PRESS

Manchester, New Hampshire

Sophia Institute Press
Box 5284, Manchester, NH 03108
1-800-888-9344

www.SophiaInstitute.com

Sophia Institute Press® is a registered trademark of Sophia Institute.

Paperback ISBN 978-1-64413-199-2

ebook ISBN 978-1-64413-200-5

Library of Congress Control Number: 2020932914

First printing

Life with Christ is a wonderful adventure.

—Pope St. John Paul II,
homily, Czech Republic, April 26, 1997

CONTENTS

FAILING FORWARD

INTRODUCTION

This book is about helping parents to form teen leaders who will lead others in their Faith and in the secular world as well.

RAISING A TEENAGER is tough enough. Add to that trying to raise a teenager who embraces his Catholic Faith, and you may feel you are facing the impossible. But as we know, or need to know, "all things are possible with God" (Mark 10:27).

To be a Catholic means, in short, to be a leader and to develop future leaders. That's what the great commandment is all about. "Go and make disciples" (read about it in Matt. 28). Jesus set up this leadership system for us right from the beginning. He picked a team of twelve Apostles whom He taught and formed to be "fishers of men" with the expectation that they, in turn, would teach and form others. It really is the perfect system for establishing the Kingdom of God and guaranteeing the future of the Catholic Church. If Jesus hadn't set up this leadership system, there would be no Catholic Church today.

That's what this book is about: helping parents to form teen leaders who will lead others in their Faith and in the secular world as well. Leadership is the cornerstone of our entire Faith. But being a leader is not an easy task. Several components are necessary for true leadership.

In this book, you will learn the step-by-step process of the CO-PEC Formation Leadership Training Method as well as examples of how these steps are implemented. COPEC stands for Challenge, Observe, Process, Evaluate, and Challenge Again. Some of these techniques may seem strange at first. Some of them might even go completely against the grain in terms of how you are raising your teenager. But don't despair; real growth happens only when there is discomfort. Eventually it will feel like second nature to you, and the future rewards will be amazing.

According to our observation and the feedback we receive from parents and teachers, teens who have been taught through our COPEC Method exhibit the following:

- ▸ greater readiness to serve, and eagerness in taking on responsibilities
- ▸ improved grades
- ▸ increased Church participation
- ▸ overall openness to constructive criticism
- ▸ a desire to work to be their best selves each day
- ▸ self-evaluation for personal effectiveness
- ▸ the ability to handle setbacks and failures more maturely
- ▸ improved decision-making skills

Your teen will learn to manifest a confidence that he can handle the challenge of a task that is given to him. He will not be afraid to fail, because he understands that failure is just a door to success. In short, he will learn *how* to be a leader.

Parents and teachers often ask us, "These results are amazing, what have you done with my child, and how can I keep this going at home?" Or, "How can I get the same results in the classroom?"

This book will help uncover answers to these questions and many more.

1

TEENS LOVE A CHALLENGE

A challenge is designed to give your teen strength—mentally, emotionally, and spiritually.

WHO EVER HEARD of succeeding through failure? It sounds a bit crazy, doesn't it? I mean, what good can come out of failing and knowing you have failed at something?

Life consistently demonstrates that growth occurs through challenges and overcoming adversity. Think about a baby who is learning to walk. The challenge of standing up, balancing, and manipulating the body through time and space is one of the earliest obstacles people overcome.

On his first attempt, the baby is far from being a marathon runner or a world-class sprinter. Yet his parents encourage him in his efforts even though he continually fails. And the baby does fail, over and over again, until he develops the necessary physical strength and skills (balance) to walk.

A challenge is designed to give your teen strength — mentally, emotionally, and spiritually. Like a baby learning to walk, your teen needs to fail over and over again until he develops the character and skills to meet and overcome obstacles consistently.

Believe it or not, your teen wants to be challenged. But what is so interesting about a challenge? Think for a second about your average teenager. He is probably interested in playing video games. Why? What makes it so much fun to play video games over and over again? The most well-known and frequently played video games are the ones that take a long time to play and have several levels and obstacles to overcome, giving the player something to achieve—a goal he can accomplish without help from an adult.

When was the last time you saw a teenager play a video game one time and then put it away forever because he did not beat the game or achieve his goal? That just doesn't happen. But why doesn't he just give up when he fails?

The philosophy behind retaining interest and active engagement is based on challenge—not only a challenge, but one your teen can complete on his own. This part is so important that we want to say it again: let him do it on his own! Not only does he not need your help to complete a task; he doesn't want it either. He wants to be able to complete these things on his own. He may be used to getting your help all the time, but that does not mean that he wants it or needs it.

If he fails on his own, he will try again. If he fails in doing things the way you demand him to do them, he will give up and expect you to step in and complete it for him. The creators of popular video games have provided an important thing that our society has taken away from our youth: a challenge he can complete on his own.

Are we saying that video games are the best way to challenge your teenager? Absolutely not. In fact, some time away from video games may be just the thing he needs in order to focus better. What we are saying is that, as a parent, you need to challenge your teen in the same manner. Give him a challenge and allow him to complete it however he wants to, without interfering with the way he approaches the challenge. It's not easy for most parents, but it is necessary if you want to guarantee your teen's future success.

By keeping your teen interested and challenged, you will enable him to achieve much more. Staying out of his way and letting him experience these challenges on his own is the only way this training works. As with video games, your teen wants to tackle challenges on his own.

Let's Get Scientific

Studies have shown that the human brain is not fully developed until around the age of twenty-five. They have also shown that around the age of eighteen, the brain is roughly halfway through the entire stage of development. The prefrontal cortex in the human brain is responsible for several key decision-making processes, such as impulse control, problem-solving, and logical thinking. Cognitive-thinking challenges help stimulate brain development and boost brain function.

One of the best ways for you to give your teen opportunities to use cognitive thinking is to challenge him frequently and let him figure out things on his own. By constantly challenging your teen, you help him to acquire good decision-making habits at a young age while his brain is in the developmental stage.

"Anything worth doing is worth doing well" is a common saying. But how can you get to the point of being able to do something well? The basis of the COPEC training method is to learn by failure. We enforce the idea that "anything worth doing is worth failing at." By allowing your teen to fail on his own, he can learn by experience and end up doing things truly well in the future!

What Do We Mean by "Challenge"?

The challenges you present to your teenager need to come with minimal rules; for example, giving only safety guidelines for things he is not to do. Aside from the safety guidelines, it is necessary to allow your teen to come up with the *how* on his own. Don't tell him how to complete the challenge at all; let him figure it out. He will not only be fine; he will surprise you and succeed on his own.

A good example of this is homework or a school project. Consider the following scenario, which you might have experienced: Your child has been assigned a project at school. He has had several weeks to complete this project, but he decided to wait until the last minute to get all the materials he needs for it. For the past three weeks, you have reminded him that it was due, but he let other things get in the way and claimed he did not have time to do it. After all, he has other homework, basketball practice, soccer practice, karate, and the school play. How can he possibly find the time to complete this project? So, at nine o'clock the night before the project is due, he asks you to drive him to Walmart so he can get his supplies. And you do it. But more than that, you feel bad for him for having to do all this work at the last minute, and you end up helping him on the project or, worse, doing it for him so he can get some sleep.

If this sounds familiar, you are not challenging your teen. You may think you are helping him by getting him through this problem, but, in fact, you are making things worse.

What should you have done in this scenario? First, it is not your job to remind your child about his school projects or homework. It is his responsibility to do it himself. Second, if he needs supplies, he should have reminded you earlier; after all, he had several weeks to get this done. But let's say, for argument's sake, that you drive him to the store to get these supplies. When you get home, it's up to him to complete the project on his own.

Can you imagine how this would look later in life for an adult? Just imagine your boss giving you a project to complete and then doing the project for you because you did not complete it. That doesn't happen in the real world. You would probably not be employed there very long if you treated work like that. Are you preparing your teen for the real world? If so, let him fail, and more than likely, he will not allow it to happen again. At least he will not make a habit of it.

This is easier said than done for most parents. Many parents try to guarantee the short-term success of their teens by doing things for them instead of allowing them to struggle a little and work things out on their own. This does much more damage, however, than allowing him to experience failure. By allowing him to fail, you guarantee his future success instead of concentrating on his immediate comfort. He will begin to recognize his strengths and weaknesses, and he will be able to correct things on his own.

What If He Fails?

Fear of failure is a learned behavior. The first time a child attempts a foot race with another child, he runs his fastest and does his best. It's only after he sees the winner of the race getting congratulated that he desires that attention and eventually becomes afraid to try. He is experiencing the fear of failure based on reactions to that failure. A teen is usually afraid to fail because he is worried about the response he will get from parents and teachers. We aren't saying that you should not demand greatness from your teen; on the contrary, we are designed in God's image and likeness—which is greatness! But demanding greatness and demanding a great outcome are two very different things.

Demanding greatness means expecting your teen to try his best at all times; to give everything he attempts 100 percent of his efforts. The outcome of these attempts will vary drastically, of course, but that does not mean that greatness has not been achieved.

For instance, if two teens are playing basketball one on one against each other and really trying their best, only one will win the game. There is always a winner and a loser. Being afraid to let your teen know he failed is lying to him. Eventually your fear is transferred to your teen. He will apply this fear to his life and not give his full effort due to the fear of failure he may experience. If your teen becomes so afraid to put forth an effort because he is afraid of failure, he will eventually turn into an unsuccessful adult who is afraid to reach his goals. Teens who are afraid even to attempt a challenge feel as though not trying equals not failing—when, in fact, not trying is failing in the first place.

Your teen needs to know that it is okay to lose when he tries his best. Losing does not mean settling for a loss; it means learning from the failure and studying, or training more effectively for the next challenge. You, as a parent, need to reinforce this thought process. That means not allowing your teen to give up when he thinks he is going to lose.

Your teen must learn to give a full effort until whatever he is doing is completely finished—just as Jesus did. Jesus did not give up on His mission. He could have come off the Cross at any time, but He chose to see it through until the end, which, of course, is really the beginning!

Taking responsibility for failure is a huge step toward emotional and spiritual maturity. Once your teen is able to say without a doubt that he did something wrong and accept the consequences that go along with it, he is much less likely to repeat that behavior in the future. After all, no one really wants to do things he knows will have negative consequences. Failure is not the problem; it's what is done with that failure that is important.

Usually parents do not allow their child to know he failed because they don't want to hurt his feelings, when, in fact, this does much more damage in the long run. By failing to acknowledge his failure, your teen will start to assign the blame to everyone else. He will say such things as "The teacher hates me," "Everyone is out to get me," "It's not fair," "It's not my fault." If you hear things like this from your teen, it is the result of not speaking the truth with love to him and letting him know that he failed.

Helping your teen look at things realistically can help. When he says, "It's not fair," help him walk through what "fair" really means: Was everyone at school assigned the project at the same time? Were you given any obstacles to overcome that no one else had to deal with? What exactly is unfair about it?

Once he realizes that he was given the exact same opportunity for success as everyone else, he can start to realize that he has been given a fair chance and that he is the problem, not everyone else. It may make you uncomfortable to hear us say, "Your child is the problem, not everyone else," but it's true. You are also part of the problem if you continue lying to him about his failures.

If parents and teachers expect teens to deal with problems head-on, then as adults we must do the same thing in our own lives. Allow your child to learn on his own.

A PARENT'S STORY

Great learning comes from experiencing failure and working through it.

THIS STORY FROM WHEN I WAS YOUNG is a perfect example of being given a challenge and failing at it. But more than that, it tells a story of great success because of the failure I experienced.

When I was about fourteen years old, I earned my Eagle Scout award in the Boy Scouts. Before I earned that rank, however, I had to face several challenges on my own and learn to overcome them. One such challenge given to me was to be in charge of a large campout that my troop was going on. I was told that I would be in charge of everything for the campout. I called the campground for reservations, made a schedule of events for the camp, made a list of people going, made sure we had enough chaperones, and determined which kids would be in charge of cooking and making the campfire, making sure all the equipment was in working order, getting all the meals prepared, and buying all the food.

My father was the scout master and allowed me to take complete control of the campout. Whenever I asked him a question about how to do something, he would say, "Am I in charge of this campout, or are you in charge?" This meant that I needed to make these decisions on my own and not ask him how something should be done.

The day of the campout arrived, and we met at the church to load all the supplies. I put myself in charge of the food because I wanted to make sure it was done right and not leave that part to chance. Food seemed to be one of the things people remembered most about our campouts, and I wanted to make it a great one. Just before getting into my father's car, he asked me if I had everything ready to go, and I told him I did. So we headed out for a three-hour drive to the campground.

Fast-forward three hours.

We arrive at camp, and I started walking around with my schedule of events, making sure everyone was doing his job, such as putting up all the tents and equipment. My father walked over to me and asked me what time dinner was planned for. I gave him a copy of the schedule and told him it would be at 6:45 p.m. so he would know what was happening as well. Then I walked over to the kitchen area and handed a schedule to the kids in charge of cooking to remind them that we had dinner planned for 6:45.

One of the kids asked me where the food was. I said, "What do you mean, where is the food?" I walked over to the trailer. No food! I looked in all the boxes we brought with us. No food! I remembered packing the food in the boxes that were inside the multipurpose room at the church before we left. I was frantically looking all around for the food when I realized that I had never packed the boxes in the trailer! I had left the food in the multipurpose room at the church. I could still picture the boxes sitting there.

I made sure everyone else was doing his job, but I had not done mine.

I walked over to my father to tell him I had messed up majorly. I told him I had left all the food behind and asked him what we should do. He said he was not sure because he was not in charge of the campout. I took a deep breath and asked him if we could go to the store and get more food. He said no because we already spent the food budget getting food. I asked him if we could either drive back to get the food or have someone bring it to us. Again, he said no because it was not anyone else's responsibility to get food; it was mine.

Frustrated, I asked my father what he would suggest, since I was out of ideas. He looked at me and said, "You said dinner was at 6:45, right?" I said, "Yes." He said, "I suggest you get dinner ready by 6:45, since everyone here is counting on you." I don't remember being speechless many times in my life, but I do remember saying nothing in return and watching him turn and walk away as if nothing had happened. He wasn't mad; he wasn't disappointed; he was just matter-of-fact with me. He told me many times before that he trusted and counted on me throughout my life, so I made a decision that I was not going to let him down.

I walked over to the kids I had put in charge of different parts of the campout and said we needed to talk. I told them I had left the food behind and let them in on the fact that we were on our own to figure this out. I asked if anyone had suggestions. At first, they were really upset with me, but after they calmed down, the suggestions started coming in. They made the same suggestions I had made to my father earlier; he had shot those down.

I told the other boys it was going to be up to us to figure this problem out and that no one was too young to help us. They finally realized that we needed to figure this out on our own. We said a prayer together for strength and wisdom and then started brainstorming ideas. We came up with a few ideas that worked really well.

One boy said we could go fishing for dinner; another boy suggested that we cut hearts of palm from the palm trees; and yet another boy said he noticed orange trees on the way to the campground and suggested we gather oranges. So we did our best to make all these things happen. In the end, we ended up catching a bunch of fish, got a ton of oranges, and found some other plants we were able to eat over the four-day campout. We figured this all out on our own without the help of any adults.

We wanted help—we even asked for it—but we ended up being allowed to experience failure, and that led to huge success. What we really wanted was to be bailed out and for someone else to take over. Even the chaperones on the trip wanted to drive and get the food for us or buy food at a local store. Fortunately, that was not allowed to happen, and I was able to learn to succeed on my own through the failure I experienced.

This is the type of challenge that cannot be simply read about. It is necessary to put these things into action and allow your teen to experience them on his own. Great learning comes from experiencing failure and working through it. What would have been learned if an adult had stepped in and bailed us out during the campout? All that would have been remembered is my failure to bring the food. We would also have remembered that an adult came to the rescue.

Where Is God in All of This?

So how does any of this relate to the spiritual growth and maturity of your teenager? Great question! Your teen needs to understand that he should never take God out of the equation. He needs to do all things with a focus on God. Without God as a focal point, no true greatness can ever be achieved.

One of the great scriptural challenges Jesus gave is when He sends out the seventy-two:

> The Lord appointed [seventy-two] others, and sent them on ahead of him, two by two, into every town and place where he himself was about to come. And he said to them, "... Go your way.... Carry no purse, no bag, no sandals; and salute no one on the road. Whatever house you enter, first say, "Peace be to this house!" ... And remain in the same house, eating and drinking what they provide, for the laborer deserves his wages; do not go from house to house. Whenever you enter a town and they receive you, eat what is set before you; heal the sick in it and say to them, "The kingdom of God has come near to you." But whenever you enter a town and they do not receive you, go into its streets and say, "Even the dust of your town that clings to our feet, we wipe off against you; nevertheless know this, that the kingdom of God has come near." (Luke 10:1–11)

What does this have to do with the way you teach leadership to your teen? Notice how Jesus sets the parameters of the challenge: He gives the objective, supplies, and basic information to complete the task. Then He sent His disciples away on their own to complete the task. He did not "helicopter parent" them or tell them exactly how to spread His Word. He only explained what He expected during the task. He also said, "First say, 'Peace to this house.'" That tells us that Jesus taught His disciples to keep God first.

Jesus gives only the parameters of the challenge. In this case, He provides some safety instructions as well, such as not to stop to greet anyone on the road, but He does not tell His disciples *how* to proclaim the Word of God. In forming your teen, remember not to tell him how to accomplish his tasks. Instead, let him learn through his experience.

Please understand, we are not saying that you should set your teen up for failure. Instead, set him up to be objective about his results. Either he accomplishes the task at hand or he doesn't. No matter the result, he needs to be told the truth and expected to deal with the outcome of his attempts. Knowing the truth will help him take ownership of those results and learn to change them on his own.

Help your teen understand that life is pass or fail. Sometimes we pass, and sometimes we fail. It's how we handle the successes and the failures that make us real leaders. It is also important for your teen to know that even in failure there is success by learning through experience. You can help him understand this by giving him a challenge and allowing him to experience everything that the challenge has to offer. All the pitfalls, obstacles, successes, and other experiences he will face will be learned on a much deeper level if he is allowed to do it on his own.

Knowing that you either did or did not accomplish whatever the task may be is invaluable. There is no such thing as kinda sorta here. In the Gospel of John, Jesus says to His disciples, "If you love me you will keep my commandments" (14:15). Jesus doesn't say, "If you love me, you'll sort of keep my commands. If you love me, you'll kind of keep my commands. If you love me, you'll intend to keep my commands." He says "you will." Jesus is saying that either you are following Him, or you are not. You are either actively working on your life as a disciple, or you are not. Jesus desires us to be intentional disciples. That means living out our faith with a purpose—and on purpose, both as parents and teens.

Having this pass-or-fail mentality reaps benefits spiritually and in our daily lives as well. For your teen to be successful, he has to have done his homework—not kinda sorta done his homework. Either he did his chores, or he did not do them. Yes or no—pass or fail.

Teaching this kind of thinking at a young age and giving young people a chance to practice it over and over sets up teens for real-world success. But a teen has to do it on his own. This is not a challenge for adults to step in and complete.

STEPS OF THE

COPEC Formation Leadership Training Method

1. *Challenge*: Give your teen a challenge.
2. *Observe*: Notice actions and inactions as your teen attempts to complete the challenge and note behaviors; don't get involved.
3. *Process*: Ask your teen questions about the decisions he made during his challenge.
4. *Evaluate*: Encourage and be honest with him about his success and failure during the challenge.
5. *Challenge again*: Based on his success or failure, give him another challenge. Maybe offer the same challenge again and give him the opportunity to do things differently this time around.

CHALLENGE

Ask your teen to
plan and cook dinner
for your family.

Let your teen take charge of everything from planning to buying groceries to cooking and timing the meal.

YOU MAY THINK WE ARE OUT OF OUR MINDS with this challenge. You may even be afraid to try it, but what are you really afraid of? Are you afraid your teen will burn your house down? Are you afraid you will be hungry and have nothing to eat? Are you already planning a backup because you do not have faith that your teen can accomplish this challenge? Well, if you are thinking any of these thoughts, stop now! Give the COPEC method a chance to work and put it into practice.

Let your teen take charge of everything from planning what he needs to purchase at the store to buying the groceries and figuring out how to cook and time the meal, right down to dessert—if he chooses to have dessert.

One note for this challenge is that you should probably let your teen know about a week or so ahead of time that he will be planning and cooking a dinner for your family. This gives him time to watch and learn how to use the kitchen equipment properly before he takes on this challenge. It is not your job to remind him he needs to learn how to use the kitchen equipment, only to let him know about the challenge and start observing his behaviors. It's up to him to ask you to show him how to use the oven if he has never used it. Just relax and observe what happens. Again, it is more than likely going to be very hard for you to step back and allow this to happen without stepping in and correcting "errors." As with everything in life, it's okay to fail—even for parents!

Let your teen figure out absolutely everything. If he has never cooked dinner, or even touched the stove before, let him figure it out. If he asks for your help concerning how to use the stove, you can show him, but don't tell him how to cook the meal he is planning. Later, in the Evaluate step, you can bring up that he could have been more effective if he had known how to use the stove prior to cooking dinner. If this scenario happens, your teen may say something like "You never showed me how to use it."

By now, you should know how to respond to a comment like that: you should tell him that it was his responsibility to learn or to ask to be shown how to use the stove since he had a week to prepare for the dinner. Don't be angry when you tell him this. Let him self-reflect (process), and he will eventually understand.

If you want to give him a budget ahead of time to set some parameters for him to follow, that's perfectly fine. If he needs a ride to the store, take him to the store—if he asks you for a ride. If he asks what he should purchase, however, remind him that he is in charge of this dinner and you are there only to drive him to and from the store (you may even want to wait in the car and allow him to go in by himself to shop). Encourage him and let him know that you have faith in him and that you know he can do this. Then let him do it completely on his own.

Once he realizes that you are not going to step in and help (and you're not!), he will see that he can use his own mind if something goes wrong, and he will learn that it's not the end of the world to fail.

Don't measure the success in this or any other task by the outcome of the dinner he cooked or how good it tasted. Success comes from your learning that your teen is capable of doing things on his own, as well as his learning that he is capable and has your support.

Encouraged independence creates future leaders. If you allow this process to work from the beginning to the end the way it is designed to work, you will see incredible strides in the maturity of your teen. Your relationship with your teen will mature and grow deeper than ever before. Trust the COPEC method, and don't give up.

2

OBSERVING MEANS WATCHING

Put prejudices or judgmental thoughts away, and simply pay attention to everything.

NOW THAT YOU HAVE GIVEN YOUR TEEN A CHALLENGE,
something for her to accomplish, it is time to observe what happens
next. This step often presents quite a bit of difficulty for parents.
Believe it or not, simply observing can be one of the hardest things
to do for many adults. Parents and teachers in general do not do
well in this area.

Adults try to protect their egos by wanting the job done right
or by sparing their teens possible negative feelings associated with a
perceived failure. In the short term, this seems good, but in the long
term, it derails the whole process of learning and accomplishment
based on self-reflection and self-improvement. It's almost as if adults
feel as though *they* have failed if their teens do not achieve a goal.

To observe effectively, it is necessary to put aside any prejudices
or judgments about *how* your teen attempts her particular challenge. In your head, you may be screaming, "You are doing it all
wrong," or "Don't do it that way!" Those are your judgments rising
up. Put those thoughts away and do your job, which is to simply
notice, and pay attention to everything.

When you observe, it is your job to notice attitudes, body
language, what is said and not said, social interaction and lack
of interaction, strategy, and approach to the task. Your goal is to

collect as much data through what you see and hear your teen doing. It is not your job to remind your teen that she needs to focus on her challenge.

Act as if you are a famous zoologist in the wild studying your favorite animal. Soak in all that your teen does and take mental notes. That is your only job at this point. As much as it irritates you to see your teen doing something differently than you would do it, resist at all costs the urge to step in and interact — other than for a safety issue. Even then, simply make your teen aware of the safety issue and leave it at that. Don't tell her how to do it differently.

We recently observed a group of parents and their children to see how they interacted during different tasks in a classroom environment. For one of the tasks, the children were asked to paint a picture of their choice. The parents were asked to sit next to their children as they painted and to observe them. That was the entire task. There were no secret instructions for the parents or the children to follow. They were simply asked to observe their children paint a picture of their choice.

Some children painted a house, a flower, or a sky with grass under it, or a combination of these things and more. The children were painting things the way they saw them, the way they thought things should be, or just plain having fun with paint and using their imaginations.

What was interesting about this experiment was that, as the children progressed in their painting, we noticed that the parents could be categorized into three groups: (1) those who told their kids how to do the task, (2) those who ignored their kids completely, and (3) those who encouraged their kids and asked questions.

With the first group, there were a lot of interruptions and directions given from the parent to the child. A parent told his child that the color the child chose for the sky was incorrect because "no one paints a purple sky." Another parent told her child not to paint the house in the picture bright green because no one would want a bright green house. Other parents even told their children to start over because they got sloppy and their paint was dripping. These parents also tended to look around at what the other kids were painting and made comments to other parents near them, almost apologizing for or excusing their own children's sloppy painting. The children of these parents tended to get frustrated and rip up their picture to start over, or quit altogether when their parents started interrupting their painting.

Then there were the parents that completely ignored their children's task and basically looked at their phones the whole time. They seemed not to be interested in the least in what was happening. These parents did not look up from their phones unless their children asked them a question or looked for approval for what they were painting. These parents did not seem to care whether their children were painting, running around the room, or even in the room at all. Their children lost interest in the painting quite often and walked around the classroom doing other things instead of finishing the painting.

The last group were parents who watched their kids paint, asked questions such as "What are you painting?" or "What color are you planning on making the flowers?" and encouraged their children without making any suggestions about how their kids should be painting. These children were not any better at painting than any of the other kids in the room, but they were much more confident, focused, and well behaved. They also did not quit painting; they stayed focused and on task the whole time.

We took notes and made our private lists about which children we thought were more emotionally mature and focused in their schoolwork and which ones seemed to struggle. But our notes had nothing to do with observing only the children; it had more to do with observing the parents' interaction with their children.

Once the challenge was done, we asked the teachers privately to point out which students seemed to be the more emotionally mature and self-sufficient and which students required more help and more attention on a regular basis.

The results we got were eye-opening, to say the least. The students whose parents asked a lot of questions about their drawings, encouraged them, and basically showed an interest in what they were doing without telling them *how* things should be done were pointed out by their teachers as the ones who displayed much more classroom and emotional maturity.

The students whose parents stared at their phones instead of being engaged with their children during the task were considered by their teachers to be less emotionally mature and less self-sufficient than those in the first group. These kids tended to be the ones who acted out in the classroom, looking for attention at all costs. They were usually the ones who got in trouble regularly and tended to be disconnected with those around them.

But the students whose parents interfered with them as they tried to figure things out on their own and paint their own pictures had the most trouble with other students, showed the least emotional stability, and had difficulty with problem-solving skills. According to the teachers, these children were the ones who expected everything to be done for them and never seemed to understand simple instructions or directions. These students also displayed a massive lack of self-assurance and constantly looked for the approval of others.

To our surprise, we were able to deduce with 100 percent accuracy which children fit into each of these categories simply by observing the behavior of the parents and watching how they interacted with their children.

One of parents' most important goals is to raise children to become stable, independent adults. Children rely on their parents for many things—from food and shelter to security and safety. As children grow, they naturally need to rely on parents less and less. As they become teens and mature into young adults, their need for independence and self-reliance increases.

The problem we see with a lot of parents is that they tend to believe that the process of moving from child to teen, and from teen to adult, is a natural process that takes place no matter what they do. Although this may happen physically, maturing emotionally and spiritually is not a natural growth process. Parents must allow space for teens to figure things out, for failure and success.

Adults should not tell a teen *how* to complete a task. The teen can and must make choices that she will be responsible for. This means that during a challenge, she is allowed to come up with her own way of doing things, even if you have never seen it done that way before. If she asks you how something should be accomplished, it is not up to you to answer that question. All you are allowed to say is, "You are in charge, and you can figure it out." Your teen needs to be empowered to do whatever it takes and make whatever decision is necessary in order to complete the challenge. She is in complete control of her success or failure, and she needs to understand that.

A PARENT'S STORY

If you want your teen to become a leader, it is essential that he or she be allowed to experience real leadership, which includes success and failure.

ONE PARENT TELLS A STORY of her teen attempting a challenge she was given and how difficult it was for her simply to observe.

I gave my daughter Wendy (fifteen) the "Make Dinner at Home" challenge. I was terrified at first. She had never had to cook anything before. When I told her about this challenge, she laughed out loud and asked me if I was serious. I explained to her that I was serious and that I had faith in her that she could do this. Then I gave her the parameters for the challenge and told her she had fifty dollars to spend on dinner for our family and that she would be making dinner on the coming Saturday. I told her it could be anything she wanted, as long as she made it herself—no fast food or already prepared meals. Again, she looked at me as if I were crazy.

I found it harder than I thought I would simply to observe her actions and inactions. Although I would have been preparing a list for the grocery store, she had nothing written down. I had to force myself to stop asking why she was doing things a certain way and from telling her to do it differently. I really didn't think I was so much of a control freak until I tried the COPEC method. Wendy never asked me how to use the oven or the stove—not even the microwave. Was she planning on asking me to buy fast food somewhere as our dinner?

Should I remind her about the rules? Should I ask her if she needs help using the oven? No. I want to stick to the COPEC method and really allow it to work. So I kept my thoughts to myself and just observed Wendy's lack of action. Her attitude seemed to be one of disbelief. Again there was a temptation to remind her that I was serious about dinner on Saturday, but I resisted.

On Friday evening, Wendy asked me if I could take her to the store to get groceries for the dinner that she was planning. Wow! I didn't think she remembered about dinner. Maybe she had been planning something all along; maybe she *could* pull this off! I am ashamed to say this, but I was actually looking for her to do things wrong at this point. I thought there was no way she would be able to handle making dinner for her family.

At the store, I told her I would wait in the car for her and then handed her fifty dollars for shopping. She thanked me and got out of the car, pausing for a moment because she still couldn't tell whether I was serious about letting her do this on her own. Then off she went into the store. I was thinking of worst-case scenarios—such as having Cheetos and apple juice for dinner. Then I considered that no one would starve and everything would be fine. I think I was trying to convince myself of this, but secretly I was still worried about not being in control.

About twenty-five minutes later, Wendy came walking out to the car with three bags of groceries. I was so tempted to ask her what we were having and then to make sure she got all the ingredients for whatever she was planning, but I resisted. I kept my questions very simple and nonintrusive, and as we were about to drive away, I asked if she got everything she needed. Wendy had this huge smile from ear to ear and told me she had it under control.

Control? I thought I was supposed to be the one in control. At home, Wendy brought the bags into the house; she hadn't let go of them since we left the store because she was so excited. She told me that dinner would be at 5:30. As she put the groceries away, I noticed spaghetti, pasta sauce, salad, salad dressing, a huge loaf of Italian bread, garlic salt and garlic butter, a chocolate cake mix, and chocolate icing. So she was going to make spaghetti? Did she know how to do that? Did she have eggs for the cake mix? Should I tell her we were out of eggs? No. I cannot interfere at this point, no matter how difficult it is for me. I just have to let her do this.

At around 4:00, I was reading a book and noticed Wendy walk past me on her way to the kitchen. She had her phone in her hand and placed it on the counter with a video running of how to cook spaghetti! I didn't say a word. I just watched her from the living room and noticed what an incredible young woman she was becoming. She was self-sufficient. Maybe I didn't need to be so controlling all the time. I watched as Wendy got a knife from the drawer and sliced the bread in half lengthwise; then she put garlic butter all over it and set is aside on a tray. She boiled the water in a large pot and put the spaghetti in the water after it started to boil. Then she pulled out another pot and put the pasta sauce in it and added salt, pepper, and garlic salt to the sauce.

I watched in amazement as she made the salad. She even washed her hands first! Where did she learn how to do this? I made sure to watch from the other room so I would not interfere with her at all. Then I watched as she put the bread into the oven, which she had preheated. About five minutes later, the spaghetti was done and she had the table set with forks, knives, napkins, and so forth — everything we needed for dinner.

She asked us all to sit down at the table and pray together before dinner. Her younger brother added that we should pray that dinner came out good! To be honest, I was thinking, "Please don't forget the bread!" But I did not say anything about it to her. We prayed and started eating the salad. So far, so good, I thought (just don't forget about the bread!). Then Wendy served the spaghetti. Excellent! It was perfectly cooked, not mushy and not undercooked. Again that thought entered into my mind: What about the bread? Then, all of a sudden, we smelled something burning. The bread!

Wendy rushed into the kitchen and came back with the burned bread in her hands, looking defeated. She said, "I really screwed this up. Just look at this bread." Her younger brother said, "It looks like charcoal!" Wendy gave him a look and tried to ignore him. I said, "Well, the bread does look a bit like charcoal, but that doesn't mean dinner is ruined."

This observing thing was really hard for me. I found myself wanting to step in throughout the process. I knew about the bread being in the oven too long. I knew it would be burned, but I didn't say anything. Does that make me an awful mother? Did Wendy learn anything from this experience? Would she ever want to try cooking again, or was this it for her because she burned the bread? I could have done this for her, and we would not have had burnt bread to eat with dinner. Maybe I should have stepped in and taken over when I knew she was about to fail. I also knew we did not have eggs at home and she didn't get any at the store, so the chocolate cake didn't happen either. Should I have said something or gone to the store to get the eggs for her while she cooked dinner? This observing thing is really hard!

The question then becomes: Is it really observing if this woman steps in to help her daughter out when she knows she is going to fail? Or would that be pretending to allow her daughter to be a leader until a really important decision comes into play and then taking over to make sure things are being done correctly? Think about that for a minute.

This is a common mistake that many adults make with teens. Adults fail to truly observe and end up taking over the task themselves, often in the name of "helping" or saying, "It's just quicker if I do it myself." This usually happens when adults see failure about to happen. Sound familiar?

How many times at home have you given your teen a chore such as vacuuming the carpet, only to take the vacuum away from her thirty seconds later because she was not doing it the way you would do it or like to see it done—or worse, micromanaging everything she did during the task? Telling her how to accomplish the task is not allowing her to learn.

If you want her to become a leader, it is essential that she be allowed to experience real leadership, which consists of success and failure. If you want her to become an adult who is fearful of making decisions and ends up being reliant on you for the rest of her life, then continue stepping in and taking over for her. If you continue giving small bits of advice or correction throughout the challenges she faces so she conforms to your vision of how things should be done, she will never have a clear vision of her own, and she will always rely on your input to answer the problems she faces.

To observe effectively, allow your teen to act on what *she* thinks should happen and how *she* wants to attempt the challenge you have given her. Save your comments for the Evaluation stage of the COPEC method. There will be time to give advice later.

If you step in and make the decision for your teen, she is not being allowed to lead. You are just pretending she is a leader, and she knows it! It's pretty hard to fool a teen when it comes to giving responsibility. She will learn quickly whether she is in charge or whether you are when you give her a task to complete.

Where Is God in All of This?

From a theological perspective, what does it mean to observe, or "keep watch"? What does it imply?

As shepherds keep watch, they look at their sheep and at the surrounding areas for danger. They watch for any pitfall that might be out there. They observe the behavior of their flock, noticing which ones are further from the rest of the flock and which ones are in the middle of the flock. The shepherd also notices which sheep the other sheep seem naturally to follow and which sheep will wander off to do its own thing. In short, the flock has freedom to make decisions and the shepherd makes sure they are safe.

The longer a shepherd owns a flock, the less guidance the flock needs. After a while, the shepherd can just be there to guide his flock gently and to keep danger away. This is how God shepherds us. He allows us to make our own decisions and write our own destinies, no matter what that might be. He allows us to be in charge of ourselves, to have free will. He doesn't interfere in our daily decisions; instead, He allows us to—we hope—learn from our experiences. He doesn't hover over us as a lot of parents do with their teens; He lets us live our lives.

God wants you to have the same type of relationship with your teen that He has with us. This translates perfectly to your teen's faith life. If you are not always there to tell her to pray or go to church, what is going to happen when she is on her own and in charge of her own faith life? It is important to observe your teen in a safe environment so you can help her process through information and evaluate her to help her grow. These important steps are covered in the following chapters, but for now, just observe!

As your teen grows in age, she needs to be allowed to grow in independence. That means allowing failure to happen and being there to observe. If you can observe her failure and allow it to happen, you can gently guide her back on the right path by allowing her time to adjust her behaviors. You will support her, but she needs to do things on her own. Otherwise, your teen will never become emotionally and spiritually mature on her own.

You probably know several adults who are emotional infants. You may even be one yourself at the moment. Emotional infants are the ones who have problems finding and keeping a job, constantly blame others for their lack of responsibility, and never understand why everyone is "out to get them." Help your teen now, when it is easier to change these damaging behaviors. You can do this by allowing her to fail without stepping in to "save" her.

OBSERVE

Without interfering, observe your teen planning a family picnic entirely on his or her own.

If you want your teen to become a leader, it is essential that he or she be allowed to experience real leadership, which includes success and failure.

Teen challenge: Ask your teen to plan completely a family picnic.

Parent challenge: Observe without interfering, helping, or interacting. That means no advice on telling your teen how to complete this task. Simply observe!

TELL YOUR TEEN that you would like her to plan a family picnic for the coming weekend. Let her know she is in charge of everything and that you trust her to make great choices. Give her a budget for the picnic, and that's all!

You are not only giving your teen a challenge but are also being given one. Your challenge is to stay out of the decision-making! Let your teen fail, even if you know she is going to fail. That does not mean that you can rub it in her face later when and if she does fail; it means only that you are allowing her to fail and to learn from it.

The questions listed below are things for your teen to figure out *on her own*. Do not give her this list of things and tell her to plan a picnic. This would not be allowing her to plan the picnic; instead, it would be making her your helper. Allow her to figure these things out, but keep this list in your mind to use later in the Process and Evaluation steps.

- ▸ What is required to plan this day?
- ▸ Where will this picnic take place?
- ▸ What route will be taken to the chosen picnic area?
- ▸ Who will attend the picnic?
- ▸ Which day will work best for the family to go on a picnic so that everyone is there together?

▸ Are there any dietary considerations that need to be addressed for those attending the picnic?

▸ How much food must be purchased for each person attending the picnic?

▸ How much will the food cost?

▸ How will the food be purchased? (By whom?)

▸ How long will the picnic be?

▸ Will games be played at the picnic?

▸ Is there anything else needed for the picnic that is not listed here?

As adults, we all know there are a lot of things not listed above that you might need to consider for a picnic. There is no mention of plates, drinks, cups, napkins, and so forth. This is where the hard part comes in. If you want your teen to grow and become a leader, you must allow her to fail. You are not causing her to fail; these decisions are hers, and she needs to be responsible for the outcome. She also needs to see how the choices she makes affects those around her as much as they affect her.

The list above outlines some necessary items for a picnic, but not all of them. If you presented this list to your teen, she would probably just check off the items and you would be on your way to a picnic, more than likely without umbrellas, bug spray, drinks, plates, cups, utensils, and so on. That means that you would probably have bugs buzzing around you and, if it rained, you would get wet. You would probably not have anything to drink at the picnic, no plates or silverware to use, and no napkins to clean up with. Guess what. That's how your teen will learn for her next challenge. Just don't do it for her! Resist the urge. You can do it!

Remember the baby we spoke of earlier in this book? If you never allowed your child to fall when she tried to walk, she would not know how important learning about balance is. She would assume that every time she was going to fall, someone would eventually catch her before she hit the ground. Now apply that thought process to your teenager. If you do not allow her to fall, she will never learn her balance in the real world.

So, as you give her this challenge, please stay out of the decision-making process. Even if you have planned a thousand picnics, and you know that things do not look right, stay out of it. Your teen will thank you later!

Here is how the challenge should go:

1. Challenge

Give your teen the picnic-planning challenge. Ask her if she understands that she is in charge of the whole picnic. Let her know that you trust her and that she will be the leader for this family picnic day.

2. Observe

Observe how she reacts to the challenge you have given her. You will probably get a lot of questions. It is your responsibility as a parent using the COPEC method to let her figure out the answers to these questions.

For instance, if her first question is "What kind of food should we have," you should respond, "You are in charge, and I am sure you will come up with something wonderful." She might respond by getting frustrated with you and rolling her eyes or by thinking your suggestion is a joke.

She may even be confused at first if you have never let her do this sort of thing before. Relax, and allow the COPEC method to work. The key to observing is just that: observe; do not instruct. Your teen needs to figure out the answers to these questions on her own.

3. Process *(More about this in the next chapter.)*
After your teen has everything planned and tells you she is ready, ask her a lot of questions about how she feels her challenge went. *Do not* ask her questions that have anything to do with her planning, such as "Did you remember to get drinks, napkins, paper plates, and so on?"

Even if you see things she has obviously not taken into consideration for the picnic, do not in any way use this Process step as a way to "fix" the things she did not do. Instead, you might ask questions such as:

▸ How did you like getting to plan the picnic?

▸ What was the hardest part about planning everything?

▸ I noticed you were frustrated with [whatever she was frustrated with]. How did you overcome your frustration or work through that problem?

▸ Which things came easy to you as you planned the picnic?

Of course, as she answers these questions, you will probably think of more questions. You might even think of questions about things she brings up. The key is to ask as many questions here as you can to understand what she was thinking and how she was acting, and not acting, during the observations you made.

Once you feel you understand what caused her to take the actions you observed, you can move on to the next stage (Evaluate) after the picnic. The Process step is very important so that you really understand how your teen thinks and feels and don't just assume you do. The more information you are able to extract from her in this step, the better.

4. Evaluate *(More about this in the next chapter.)*

This step should be done after the picnic. You should evaluate not only your teen's performance in planning the picnic but also the planning process itself. In this stage, you will still ask questions, but you will also give advice—with love. Giving advice does not mean telling your teen that she did things wrong in comparison with the way you would have done them. Giving advice means suggesting that maybe next time she could do things differently based on the information *she* gave *you* earlier.

If the planning process was very hectic for her, for instance, and you noticed that she handled things well even though she was frustrated, let her know. Tell her that you saw that she was frustrated and know she had a tough time, but you are proud of how well she handled it. On the other hand, if she did not handle the frustration well, let her know that as well. Tell her you think she can handle frustration better than she did and you expect more from her because she is great and made in the image of Greatness. Speak the truth with love! But be honest about failure and success.

Sometimes teens are afraid to try because they are afraid to fail. Let your teen know you are happy that she tried, and ask her if she tried her absolute best. Did she do everything she could to make things successful? If she answers honestly that she did her best, congratulate her—even if the picnic was a horrible failure and things did not go smoothly at all. This step is where you get to put your two cents in. Just make sure you are giving her credit and letting her know that she did fail (if there was a failure) and that it is okay to fail.

Don't pretend that everything was great if it wasn't. Keep an up-beat attitude, even when discussing her failure and she will be more likely to try and fix the failure on her own next time as opposed to not trying again because she doesn't want to disappoint you.

5. Challenge Again *(More about this in the next chapter.)*
Quickly give her another challenge. If she failed at a part of this challenge, give her the opportunity to fix it now. Don't wait. And be very clear about when you would like this done. Pick a date, possibly the next weekend or day off. Ask her what she would do differently the next time.

If she tells you she would choose a better place, or plan to bring napkins or paper plates next time, then challenge her to plan another picnic and try to fix everything she feels went wrong the first time. This accomplishes a few very important things:

▸ It lets her know not to give up when she doesn't achieve perfection the first time.

▸ It shows her you still have faith in her and still see her as capable of being a leader.

▸ It allows her to have another opportunity to be seen as a leader even though she failed the first time around.

Remember to stay out of her decision-making process all the way through, as with the first challenge. After the Challenge Again step, work your way through the whole process again, right down through the Evaluate step. Your teen will look forward to these challenges if you give them often.

3

GIVE TIME TO PROCESS

Processing forces the issue of confronting one's feelings, attitudes, assumptions, behaviors, and judgments.

NOW THAT YOU HAVE LAID OUT THE CHALLENGE for your teen and observed him in action, it's time to do something with all the data you've gathered. This brings us to the third step: Process.

Processing information is one of the most critical steps in the COPEC method. In fact, this step is so important that it can make or break the entire system. This step can deepen trust and relationships between parent and teen. In a lot of ways, the Process step is another way of telling your teen, "I love you, and you matter to me." When you invest time and energy in this area, you will reap the benefits of understanding how your teen thinks, what his worldview looks like, and how he perceives your relationship with him.

Warning: this step doesn't always *feel* comfortable when you work with teens, but that doesn't matter; you are here to grow, and growing isn't always comfortable. One of the biggest challenges for a parent is to slow down conversations and create time to process with your teen. Usually this step is more uncomfortable for teens than it is for adults. The Process step forces teens to be self-reflective.

What exactly is the Process step, and what does it involve? Processing forces the issue of confronting one's feelings, attitudes, assumptions, behaviors, and judgments. Processing allows the teen to voice his thoughts, feelings, and opinions in a safe, respectful environment.

The Process step is vital, as it allows your teen to make sense of the experience and gives him time to learn how to self-reflect. In this step, your teen will:

▶ Reflect on his experience and on the outcome of his challenge.

▶ Reflect on his actions and inactions.

▶ Communicate his experience to you, the parent.

Furthermore, this step is a valuable tool for demonstrating the communal aspect of living. Processing illuminates for your teen how his behaviors affect his neighbors (positively or negatively). Instead of thinking only about himself and how his actions affect him, the Process step forces your teen to think of how others are affected by his actions as well.

To implement this step of the COPEC method effectively, you, as the parent, must put aside any judgment and focus merely on the behavior that contributed to the success or failure of the challenge. Put aside any preconceived "story" you are telling yourself. If you put aside your personal feelings and listen, you will begin to hear the way your teen thinks. This is not about agreeing with his point of view, as those views can sometimes be very extreme. Rather, it's about understanding his perspective.

An easy way to remember the meaning of Process is to remember the phrase "Process = Perspective."

When the Process step is successful and done well, you, as a parent, are sending a very strong message to your teen and that is: "I care about you and your viewpoint." This is invaluable to parents if they are to keep their teen growing in the Church and actively engaged. Again, it does not mean you have to agree, just that you are willing to listen to the viewpoint of the teen without dumping hundreds of reasons on him that he is wrong for thinking the way he does. If your teen feels truly heard, and knows without a doubt that his thoughts, opinions, and views matter to you, he will keep opening up to you.

Parents often mistake the Process step for telling their teen what he should know or how he should think. Not only is this counterproductive, but it will create more problems down the road.

The goal of the Process step is to assist your teen to articulate the events, thoughts, and feelings of his experience during his Challenge. It is the parent's job simply to understand—not necessarily to agree, but simply to understand. So ask a lot of questions to gain that understanding. St. Francis of Assisi said it best: "O Master, grant that I may never seek so much … to be understood as to understand."

One of the great benefits of the Process step is that it puts your teen in a position to receive feedback about his behavior in a nonjudgmental manner. Successful processing of information with your teen will help him to self-reflect and to become more effective in his interactions with you.

This is often a new experience for teens, as many are used to having their attitudes and thoughts judged by adults, especially their parents. As parents, you are called to judge actions and behaviors, not people. Allowing your teen to process his actions helps drive this point home when you listen to what he has to say and truly try to understand him.

Processing can be very difficult for teens as they struggle to separate personal judgments and their behavior. But this is an ongoing skill that must be developed if parents want to raise successful leaders.

A common process question that parents often ask teens, albeit out of frustration is, "What were you thinking?" This is a great question when presented in the COPEC method, which requires an attitude of curiosity, not judgment. This type of question, said without anger or attitude, becomes a relationship-enhancing question.

Your teen may say he wasn't thinking at all and most likely he made an impulse decision, but the question alone moves him closer to adulthood by getting him to think about things he wasn't "thinking about."

Because the Process step focuses on self-reflection, it also helps teens to examine their consciences, an important part of the sacrament of Reconciliation. A leader needs to be honest with himself when things are not working or are going wrong. He needs to have the ability to look objectively at his faults, not from condemnation, but from the lens of effectiveness and Christian virtue.

A PARENT'S STORY

The COPEC method was working and helped my son to process his thoughts and feelings.

THE FOLLOWING STORY comes from speaking to a parent about his son's failing a test at school. The father in the story does a great job helping his son process why he failed his test at school.

Earlier this year, I started implementing the COPEC method with my two sons. My younger son, Nate (fourteen), was having some trouble with math, and after meeting with his teacher several times, I came to the conclusion that the issue here was with my son, not with the teacher.

It all started when Nate failed a math test at school and blamed it on his teacher. I don't like when he blames others, and I had noticed him doing it more and more. I needed to put a stop to this "victim mentality" before it became a problem. That was when I started to implement the COPEC method at home. I asked Nate why he thought he failed his test. His answer was that his teacher did not tell him about the test and that it was unfair because all the other kids in the class knew about it.

Instantly, I wanted to get upset with him and ask why all the other kids knew about the test except for him. I tried my best to remain silent, as the COPEC method outlines for this step. I asked him if there was anything else he wanted to tell me about why he failed the test. He said that he just didn't have time to study because of baseball practice after school and all his other homework. He said he didn't understand why his teacher didn't like him and that he tried his best at school, but no matter what he did, his teacher seemed to pick on him.

I said I wanted to make sure I understood how he was feeling, so I repeated back to him exactly what he told me and said, "If I understand you correctly, you feel that your teacher picks on you and does not offer you the same opportunities that the other students are given when taking tests in his class. Is that right?" Nate sat there for a second and thought about what I asked him. He said, "I do feel he picks on me, but I guess I have the same opportunities as everyone else usually."

I asked him what he meant about having the same opportunities, and he told me that the teacher usually writes the test date on the board in the classroom, but that Nate didn't realize it was there. So I asked him if he felt it was the teacher's responsibility to make sure each student individually reads the board and knows when the test is going to take place, or if that is the students' responsibility. Nate told me that it was the students' responsibility but that he still felt as though he was being picked on by the teacher.

I asked Nate to explain what he meant by being picked on. He told me that the teacher gave him extra work that most of the other students did not have to complete because, in order to raise his grade, he needed more practice with the problems he was struggling with. Nate said it wasn't fair that the teacher was singling him out when most of the other students didn't have the extra homework.

Again, I told Nate I wanted to make sure I understood what he was saying about being picked on by the teacher, so I repeated back to him what I heard him say. I said, "If I understand you correctly, you are upset because the teacher is giving you extra homework to help you improve your grades when most of the other students don't have to do this extra work. Is that correct?"

Nate said, "Well, yes, that is right, but he is not giving me extra work just to help me improve my grades; he is picking on me." I asked him to explain a little more for me because I did not understand exactly what he was upset with the teacher about. Nate sat there quietly for a second and then finally said, "I guess he is giving me the extra work only to improve my grades, but I just don't want to have to do this work."

Okay, I thought, I can see this process working! I asked Nate to think about why he was really upset and whom he was upset with. He told me he was upset that he had to do the work. Again I asked him whom he was upset with. Nate said, "I guess I am upset with myself because I wish I was better at math and didn't have to do the extra work."

I really did not expect Nate to say those words. I honestly expected to have a long, drawn-out battle trying to get him to realize that this was not the teacher's fault. I think the reason it worked so well was that Nate came to this realization on his own. I didn't tell him what the answer was; he figured it out by using logical thinking and by communicating his feelings. I was also able to understand that I might take for granted how I had to work through this process myself when I was his age.

I asked Nate to think about his original statement—that the teacher was picking on him—and whether he still thought he was being picked on. He said, "No, I guess he is only trying to help me improve my grades. It's my fault that I have to do this work to begin with." I asked him what he thought he could do to improve his grades so he would not have to do this extra work any longer. He sat there quietly for about a full minute just thinking and finally said, "I could probably put a little more time into studying and a little less into being on my phone before I go to bed at night." What? Who was this kid, and what just happened, I thought. The COPEC method was working and helped my son to process his thoughts and feelings. It also helped me communicate more effectively and slow down to really understand how he was feeling.

Now if I could just get him to clean his room more often! Maybe I'll use the COPEC method to help me understand why his room is so messy all the time. One challenge at a time!

Where Is God in All of This?

There are two great examples of this sort of processing in the New Testament. The first is the story of Philip and the Eunuch. Acts 8:26–40 tells us that the Apostle Philip has just left Jerusalem and is headed for Gaza. He meets an Ethiopian who held a high position in the court of Candace, queen of Ethiopia. The Ethiopian was leaving Jerusalem and heading back to his homeland to report back on his finding on Judaism.

When Philip comes upon him, the Ethiopian is reading the book of Isaiah. Philip approaches the man and asks if he understands what he is reading. The man replies, "How can I unless someone explains it to me?" He invites Philip to join him, and on the journey they take together, a better understanding is reached. The journey is the Process that Philip uses to speak to the man about Jesus.

Philip doesn't force his views upon the man, nor does he command that the man be saved, or baptized. Yet, in the end, the Ethiopian asks Philip to baptize him. What's most important is that Philip took *time* to ask, listen, and understand. The Process step likewise requires time, but what a great way to show your teen you love him by giving him your time. Time is something you cannot get back once it is gone, so make the most of every minute with your teen.

The instance of "Process" is also found in the Gospels of Matthew, Mark, and Luke. Here, Jesus sends out His disciples (He challenges them). They cure the blind, heal the lame, and cast out demons.

In Mark 6:7–13, 30, we read:

And he called to him the twelve, and began to send them out two by two, and gave them authority over the unclean spirits. He charged them to take nothing for their journey except a staff; no bread, no bag, no money in their belts; but to wear sandals and not put on two tunics. And he said to them, "Where you enter a house, stay there until you leave the place. And if any place will not receive you and they refuse to hear you, when you leave, shake off the dust that is on your feet for a testimony against them." So they went out and preached that men should repent. And they cast out many demons, and anointed with oil many that were sick and healed them.... The apostles returned to Jesus and told Him all that they had done and taught.

Jesus challenged His disciples and said, "Go out to the towns and preach the good news, carry nothing but the clothes on your back." Needless to say, the Apostles came back talking about their experience. When they came back, they told Jesus everything about their challenge; they shared with Him. They were self-reflecting on the situations they were in and how they were able to deal with them with God's help.

Reading this story, most people gloss over the most important part. What did Jesus do? He listened! He allowed His disciples to share their experience, to enter into their experience, to see things from their perspective as it happened, and to understand what it meant to them. That is the purpose of the Process step: to accompany your teen on the journey and allow him to walk you through his thinking without judgment or condemnation. Allow him to self-reflect and come to his own conclusions.

4

EVALUATE: SPEAK THE TRUTH WITH LOVE

Giving an honest evaluation means telling the truth and giving encouragement to keep trying in order to improve.

HOW MANY TIMES have you been to a sporting event or a recital to watch your teen perform when she had an absolutely horrific performance or played the worst game you have ever seen her play? Chances are, you probably uttered those two words that many parents say to their child after such an event: "Good job" or "Good game." Even worse, other parents and other children on the team probably said it to your teen as you were leaving.

Saying "Good job" when the job clearly wasn't good is a lie. You may have the best intentions in the world when you say it, but the fact is that those words are a big, fat lie! Parents tend to argue this point by saying that their intention was not to tell their children they did a good job during the game but to tell them they did a good job in their effort, or that they even showed up for the game. But even this can be a lie, mainly because of how it is received. Your child is likely not thinking you meant that she did a good job by showing up and trying; instead, she takes your comment to mean that she did a good job with her performance in the game, which she probably knows is not true.

This sends a dangerous message to your teen. It tells her that just by showing up, she has done what is required to be successful. As she grows into an adult, this message is applied to the way she approaches a career, relationships with friends and colleagues, and relationships with her future spouse as well. It is important that your teen hears you speak the truth. If she hears you speak the truth, she will speak the truth as well.

Are we saying you should tell your kid she blew the game? No, of course not. But praise needs to be specific. For example, if your teen has a horrible game, you might ask her, "How do you think you did today?" She will probably know she didn't do so well. It's important for her to know that it is okay to have a bad game, to mess up, and not to be perfect. Acknowledging the fact that she didn't do well and that life will still go on is very important. If you choose to give praise for something, you can always let your teen know you are proud of her for not quitting. But saying her performance was a "good job" is just not true, so don't say it.

Giving an honest evaluation does not mean that you have to tell your teen she did a horrible job. On the contrary, it means that you can give her encouragement to keep on trying and practicing to keep improving. Just don't lie to her about anything in the process. If she failed, she needs to know the truth.

GRANDMA'S COOKIES

In this story, Grandma responds with honesty and keeps things clear and nonjudgmental.

IT IS EXTREMELY IMPORTANT for parents and teachers to give teens honest evaluations. The following story gives an excellent example of the Evaluate process.

Two teenage girls were spending the day with their grandmother. They loved their grandmother's cookies and always asked her to bake them when they spent the day together. This time, the girls asked their grandmother if they could bake the cookies.

The grandmother thought about the request for a second, then got her recipe book and handed it to the girls. She told them that they were welcome to use the kitchen to bake the cookies and told them to follow the recipe exactly as it was written if they wanted the cookies to turn out the same as when she made them.

The girls read the recipe, which was handwritten and very old. They took three eggs out of the refrigerator and put them on the counter. They got two cups of flour and all the other ingredients together and placed them on the counter. They saw that the recipe called for "3/4 cups of sugar." Because the numbers were written side by side, the girls thought it meant to add three or four cups of sugar, instead of three-fourths of a cup of sugar.

After the girls combined the ingredients, they put the cookies on the cookie sheet and placed them in the oven. In about fifteen minutes, the first batch of cookies came out of the oven. The girls were excited to have baked the cookies, which smelled delicious, and equally excited to have their grandmother taste the cookies. They put three cookies on a plate, poured a glass of milk, and then called their grandmother to come and taste the cookies.

Their grandmother came and sat at the kitchen table and told the girls how wonderful the cookies smelled all through the house. She told the girls she could not wait to taste the cookies and how proud she was of them for making them all by themselves without any help. Then their grandmother took a bite of a cookie. Instantly, she knew something was not right. She finished chewing and swallowed the first bite as the girls watched her face for her approval. The girls asked their grandmother how she liked the cookies. Their grandmother thought for a second and then she spoke.

She told the girls that the cookies did not taste right and that something must have not been followed correctly in the recipe. The girls got the recipe book and went through step by step with their grandmother, telling her what they did during the process. Finally, they came to the sugar portion of the recipe, and instantly the grandmother knew what they had done wrong. Lovingly, she explained that it was not three or four cups of sugar they were supposed to add but three-fourths of a cup of sugar.

The girls and their grandmother all laughed at the mistake and decided it would be best to scrap this batch and start again. So the grandmother told the girls to give it another try, which they did, and the cookies came out perfectly the second time.

You may be thinking, "So what?" Two girls made some cookies the wrong way, and their grandmother said she didn't care for them. Big deal, right? What does this story have to do with evaluating?

Think for a second about the grandmother's response when the girls asked if she liked the cookies they made. She responded with honesty and kept things clear and nonjudgmental. She did not get upset with the girls because the cookies came out wrong. *She spoke the truth with love.* That's the key to the Evaluate step of the COPEC method. Speak the *truth* with love.

What would have happened if the grandmother, instead of being honest with the girls, told the girls that their cookies were perfect because she was trying not to hurt their feelings? The girls would have tasted the cookies and known instantly that their grandmother had not been honest with them. What good would that have done? The repercussions may not have been instant, but the girls would have known that their grandmother was not always honest with them. This might have given the girls the idea that they would not have to be honest with their grandmother either.

It might also have led to future problems, as the girls might have stopped asking their grandmother for her opinion if they thought she was going to lie to them. Worse yet, they might ask for their grandmother's input only when they knew they would hear something seemingly favorable.

You may not think you are lying to your teen when you tell her she has done a good job, but think about what you are telling her. What exactly was good about it? Think specifics here.

Are you telling her she did a good job because you want to soften the harsh reality of a poor performance, or do you really believe the performance was a good one? Usually this lie is told because no parents want to see their children feel bad. Parents say these things to create warm and fuzzy feelings—at least for the moment. But this really does more damage than good. Your teen already knows the truth about her performance. She needs to be encouraged by you. Let her know that she didn't perform too well but that you know she will figure out a way to improve next time. If she does not know she failed, how can she improve?

Parents need to be able to offer criticism constructively and in a controlled environment. You only have your teen's best interests in mind, so be honest with her and let her know exactly what she already knows—the truth about her performance.

Often, a teen expects the Evaluate step to be the one in which her parents get to tell her how she should have gone about completing the challenge. This is *not* the goal of the Evaluation step. Please make sure you understand this point. If you end up telling your teen how to complete a task, then expect her to do it your way the next time she tries something on her own. She will then be doing things the way you expect them to be done and not on her own. So who is the real leader if she is doing what you command? Think about it.

You are not evaluating right or wrong. You are not evaluating the success or failure of the outcome of her challenge. You are only evaluating her actions during the challenge on the basis of the information she gives you during the Process step.

The key to the Evaluate step is to speak the truth with love. You are allowed to criticize or judge only your teen's actions during the challenge—*never* your teen herself. It's okay to judge the actions and intentions behind her performance, as long as you speak the truth with love.

The distinction between Process and Evaluate can be blurry. To clarify, in the Process step, your teen talks about her experience during the challenge. The Evaluate step is a discussion between you and your teen about the effectiveness of her efforts. It considers not only whether the challenge was completed successfully but also what the circumstances and intentions were behind your teen's actions. It helps for you to explore all the factors that went into the decisions that were made in completing the challenge. Criticize, appraise, and judge the actions, not the person.

As your teen moves through the Evaluate step, she will become more open to criticism and judgment, both in giving and receiving, because she will realize that the focus is on her performance, not who she is as a person. Eventually your teen will look forward to hearing her evaluations because she will know that you are speaking the truth out of love for her. She will also look forward to improving herself, not only for your satisfaction, but her own.

The Evaluate step prepares teens for real-world experience. Many business owners have performance reviews for employees rising through the ranks into management. Think of this as a performance review for your teen rising into adulthood. This will also help her learn not to be too thin-skinned and to accept criticism.

A PARENT'S STORY

A father's evaluation gives confidence because the son was able to overcome obstacles on his own.

ONE DAD TELLS HIS STORY of giving an honest evaluation to his son and how it helped form him as he matured.

My son is a great kid. He means the world to me, and I want to be able to provide everything he wants so he doesn't feel as if he is missing out on anything that other kids have. But I noticed that he started acting a little "entitled." I don't think he was doing this intentionally. I think that, because he never had to work for anything, he didn't realize the value of the things he had.

One day he came to me and told me he would like to get a new bike because he was outgrowing his old one. I thought for a minute and then told him I thought he should earn money for the new bike. He said, "Seriously? It's not that expensive. I don't understand why I have to earn the money for the bike myself. My friend just got a new bike, and he didn't have to work for it."

I looked at him and said, "Haven't I always given you whatever you wanted?" He said, "I guess so." I said, "Well, think about it: is there anything you need that I have not provided you with?" He said, "No, I have everything I need ... except for the new bike I want." I said, "It sounds as if this bike is really something you want, so I am going to help you get it. It is important for me as a father to provide you with what you need, both now and for your future. There is one thing I have not given you that I know you will need as you get older, and I would like to give this to you now." He said, "What is it?"

I said, "I am going to give you the gift of understanding value. You said you wanted a new bike, and I am going to make sure you have the opportunity to get one." He said, "What do you mean?" I think he could tell I was up to something, but he wasn't sure exactly what quite yet. I said, "I am going to give you an opportunity to earn your own money for this bike. You may not understand it right now, but this will be the best gift I could possibly give you." He said, "I have to earn my own money for the bike? I don't need a new bike that bad. Just forget it." I said, "No, I am not going to forget it. You are going to earn the money you need for this bike on your own, and I am going to be here to help keep you on the right track."

Rolling his eyes, he said, "Okay, what do you want me to do?" I said, "That's not how this works. You are going to have to figure out how to make the money yourself. I cannot help with any part of this, but I will be here for support. You can do it, and I believe in you."

Now that I had given him the challenge, I was going to observe his reaction to the challenge. This challenge went on all summer. I noticed that at first, he did some yard work for a few neighbors to get money. Then he ran out of gas for the lawnmower and asked me for money to get gas. I told him that he would have to use the money he earned for gas money. He was frustrated, but he took the lawnmower and walked up to the corner store to get gas. On his way back, he stopped at the house next to the gas station and asked if they had any yard work that needed to be done.

They told him they didn't, but they needed their shed painted. So he ended up painting their shed. Then their neighbor needed a few things done. This is the way his whole summer went. He went from one neighbor to another, and with the money he earned, he even had flyers made to pass around our neighborhood.

Once his efforts started paying off, his attitude changed a great deal. With two weeks of summer vacation left, and after working his fingers to the bone all summer, he finally had enough money for the bike he wanted. He asked me for a ride to the store to get the bike, and I gladly obliged. When we got the bike home, he was happier than I had ever seen him with any gift he had received from me, or from anyone else, for that matter.

I asked him how he felt having earned the money for the bike without my help. He said it made him grateful for all the things I have given him and that he was sorry if he ever took me for granted or didn't seem to appreciate me. He said he appreciated the bike even more because he earned it and realized how hard it was to work for a goal.

I told him I was very proud of him for not giving up. I also told him that I noticed how his attitude changed from the beginning to the end of the challenge. He said he didn't know what I meant. I told him that when I gave him the challenge of having to earn his own money for the bike, he was frustrated that I just didn't get him the bike. Then, as he worked mowing lawns and ran out of gas for the lawn mower, I told him I noticed that he was frustrated with me for not providing the gas money. I told him that once he paid for the gas himself and was able to do even more work, I noticed that his work habits started to improve.

I told him how great it was to see his attitude change when he started seeing some success. I told him that it was very clear that once his attitude changed, he started enjoying the work he was doing. But my favorite thing of all was to see how proud of himself he was when he got the bike he earned all by himself.

To this day, my son earns all his own money on the weekends by doing chores around the neighborhood and has a few friends helping him too. He is even considering opening his own full-time business when he gets older. I know that my encouragement throughout his challenge played a big part in helping him become a well-rounded and effective leader.

This is a great evaluation from a loving father to his son. It shows that although there were some obstacles for his son to overcome, his son overcame them without any help from anyone. It also shows that the father pointed out an early failure, and the son was able to deal with knowing he failed during the challenge and was able to overcome it on his own.

Where Is God in All of This?

The Evaluate step can be a great opportunity to say: "I care about you enough to speak the truth about your performance. I care enough about you to tell you the truth about what I perceive went well and what areas held you back."

There is a common misconception in society about judging. People often misinterpret the Bible verse "Judge not, lest you be judged" (see Matt. 7:1) to mean that a person's behavior should not be questioned. We are, however, called to judge actions and situations. That means we need to scrutinize the rightness or wrongness of behaviors and ideas.

True, we cannot judge like Jesus, who judges a person in terms of his worthiness of heaven, but Proverbs 31:9 tells us to judge fairly. The point of the Evaluate step is to judge fairly the effectiveness of the actions, attitudes, and intentions of the teen, not the teen as a person.

To put this in perspective, think about what would happen if you were at a store with a friend of yours and you saw that friend walk over to a jewelry counter, grab a handful of jewelry, and try to run out of the store. Your first response would probably be to say, "What do you think you're doing? Put that back! You know stealing is wrong!" Are you judging the friend's behaviors? Absolutely!

This type of judgment keeps us from doing wrong and helps us to discern what is right and wrong.

It's no different when you point out right and wrong behaviors in your teen. Start teaching by example and show your teen how to speak the truth with love and how to keep her focus on God. Imagine what the world would be like if everyone, at all times, spoke the truth out of love for one another.

5

DON'T STOP NOW: CHALLENGE AGAIN

In life, we are always challenged. In this way, the Challenge Again step simulates life.

HOW MANY PROFESSIONAL ATHLETES do you know of who do not practice? How do you think they got to be a professional in the first place? A famous professional basketball player said, "I am not the most talented guy out there, but I am the guy that practices hardest. That makes all the difference in the world when push comes to shove."

Anything successful in life takes time and practice. The CO-PEC method is no different. Give it time, and keep challenging your teen. Do it again and again. Don't give up. It may seem that nothing is changing and that your teen just isn't making progress, but in reality the COPEC method will be working. Growth takes time, so give it time and be patient.

Think of practicing the COPEC method like planting a seed. If you plant the seed, water it, fertilize the soil, and give it enough sunlight, you probably won't see any growth the first day. You may not even see growth the second or third day, but the perseverance of watering, fertilizing, and providing sunlight is doing something. Then one day, after much repetition, you see small results—a literal breakthrough as the plant sprouts. Likewise, you may not see the changes in your teen immediately, but by using the COPEC method over and over again, you will see results that will help your teen become better formed in his faith and in living a life that is focused on God.

Teens need ongoing challenge, whether large or small. It can be a challenge you plan way ahead of time, or a challenge to keep your teen working through something he is struggling with to figure out how to overcome it. If you give your teen only one challenge and then never do this again, how can you expect to see great results? Don't give up, and don't let your teen give up either. He will follow your example in how he approaches a challenge. Don't underestimate the ability of your teen to accomplish a task you give him, even if he fails miserably the first time around. Without being given another opportunity, how can he make changes that end in success?

The main problem adults have with the Challenge Again step is that parents panic when something goes wrong during the original challenge and refuse to make that same mistake again. How ironic! Teens will amaze you with their abilities to adapt. All you need to do is give your teen the opportunity to grow, learn, and develop, again and again, even after incredible failure!

The main problem teens have with the Challenge Again step is that they feel that they have disappointed their parents. This is why encouraging your teen through his failure is so important. Recognize the failure, then encourage him to grow past it.

The Challenge Again step simulates life. As adults, we know that life is full of challenges. We are always being challenged. We are either just beginning a challenge, in the middle of one, or about to end one. That's life. This is what you want to simulate for your teen to prepare him to handle the challenges life will give him.

Sometimes the same challenge repeats itself until we develop the necessary skills, understanding, and strength to navigate that obstacle successfully. An unskilled bike rider will face the challenges of maintaining balance, stopping, and pedaling over and over again, until he can successfully do these things on his own.

A PARENT'S STORY

A mother acknowledges failure, encourages her son, and presents him with another challenge in which he can improve.

A MOM SHARES her Challenge Again success story and how her evaluation helped her son want to improve himself.

After the "Plan a Picnic Challenge," I wanted to throw this book away and never challenge my son with anything else ever again. What a disaster! He didn't bring any drinks, plates, or bug spray. We were sitting there in misery the whole time with a half-full bottle of mustard, stale bread, a half-eaten bag of potato chips, and a ridiculous number of mosquitoes.

I was about finished with letting my son plan anything. But I knew I would be frustrated with this process, as I am a bit of a control freak. That's the great thing about this COPEC method: it makes you take a look at your own life as well. Anyway, I wanted to quit, but I didn't, because I wanted to give COPEC a chance to work. So, after the picnic, I asked my son how he thought the picnic went. I asked what he would have done differently if he had to do it over again. Then I tried to remain calm and listened to what he had to say.

He said he would make sure he took the challenge seriously the next time around. I asked why he didn't take it seriously this time. His answer shook me a bit. He said, "I really thought you were going to step in and get food at the last minute, so I didn't put a whole lot of thought into what I was bringing for food. I picked this place near the lake because I was honestly a little upset with you for not getting any food and putting this all on me, and I thought this place would be full of mosquitoes. I'm sorry."

Whoa! Did my son tell me he was trying to sabotage the picnic he was supposed to be in charge of? Did he admit that he was trying to make me miserable? Okay, well I had a couple of choices to make. First, I could react as I normally would and start yelling at him—which closes him off and makes for a horrible feeling when we are finished arguing. Or, I could keep trying to work through the CO-PEC method and realize he just processed what happened. Maybe this is a good thing.

Instead of getting upset and yelling, I chose to try to give an honest evaluation. I started by telling him that I noticed that he did not put very much thought into the picnic. I told him I was disappointed that he would choose this place for a picnic, not because it was a bad choice, but because he did it deliberately to upset me. I also told him that I was sure that if he put as much thought into planning this picnic as he did into sabotaging it, he would have planned a great picnic. He asked me if I was upset with him for trying to ruin our picnic.

I kept thinking of the COPEC method and how parents are encouraged to ask a lot of questions, so I asked him why I would be upset. He said, "Well, I would be upset if I were you. I tried to ruin everything because I didn't want to be here." I said, "I am not upset with you for being honest with me. I love that you told me the truth. But I am a bit disappointed that you chose not to take advantage of a great opportunity to show me how responsible you can be. I hope you understand the difference."

My son said, "I do understand. I really felt awful about it when the mosquitoes started swarming." We packed everything up and headed for the car, and as we were packing the trunk with our picnic supplies, I asked my son, "If you had the chance to do this again, what would you do differently?" He said, "Well, I would take it seriously and really plan the picnic. I would also not choose the same place for the picnic."

I said, "Okay, then show me. Plan another one for next Saturday." He looked at me as if I were crazy and said, "Are you serious? You are going to trust me to do this again after everything I just told you?" I said, "Of course. Everyone makes mistakes, but not everyone gets a second chance to improve all the time. In this case, I am giving you another opportunity to take charge and make it happen next weekend, to fix whatever mistakes you think you made and really give it a full effort. I know you can do it, but you have to believe you can as well." He said, "Awesome! Thanks, Mom. I won't let you down this time. I may screw something up, but I am really going to try my best."

This is a great example of not saying "Good job" when a good job was not done. This mother could have said she was proud of her son for trying, but he really didn't try. She handled it great and kept encouraging her son by telling him she trusted him and that everyone makes mistakes. She acknowledged the failure and didn't pretend that it didn't happen. Without her giving him another challenge, the last thing her son would remember is that he messed up and that his mom didn't give him any more opportunities to improve. He would have thought she did not trust him and would have hidden his future failures from her because he would have felt that she would not understand. Now he knows she does.

Where Is God in All of This?

Reading the Gospels, you will notice that Jesus continually challenges His disciples and talks a lot about seeds, farming, planting, and so forth. Why farming? Well, Jesus must be trying to tell us something important here!

Sometimes the challenges He gives his disciples are different because they finally got what He was teaching. There was, however, one broad challenge that Jesus posed to His disciples over and over because they didn't quite get it until the end, and even then they didn't get it fully. That challenge was to accept that He (Jesus) had to die and then rise again. The Apostles didn't understand that Jesus would need to suffer and die. In the Gospel of Matthew, we read: "From that time Jesus began to show his disciples that he must go to Jerusalem and suffer many things from the elders and chief priests and scribes, and be killed, and on the third day be raised" (16:21).

Peter tries to stop Jesus (clearly not accepting the challenge). Jesus firmly rebukes Peter, saying, "Get behind me, Satan! You are a hindrance to me; for you are not on the side of God, but of men." Even as Jesus was dying on the Cross, the Apostles didn't get it, as evidenced by their leaving Jesus alone to die (except John and Mary, Jesus' Mother).

But consider that Jesus repeatedly told the Apostles, then showed them, and then in the Resurrection showed them again.

Eventually they got it and, at Pentecost, filled with the Holy Spirit, went out and conquered the challenge and truly "made disciples of all nations" (see Matt. 28:19).

If you constantly challenge your teen, he will start to take control of his own life. Keep challenging him spiritually as well, and if there comes a time that he does not agree with a certain teaching, he will not give up on his Faith. He will work through it on his own. He may ask you for advice, or question you about his Faith, but this is a good thing. Too often, teens come to a teaching they do not agree with in the Catholic Faith and then decide to look for a church that agrees with their way of thinking—or stop going to church altogether. Challenging your teen again when he fails sets up a "Don't quit—won't quit" attitude that will transfer to all parts of your teen's life, even his faith life!

Take a moment to reflect on areas of your teen's life. Find a challenge that he didn't get and consider making that his Challenge Again. One word of caution: don't expect miracles overnight. You many need to present this challenge to him once a month or once a week. Maybe it's a daily challenge that you need to present until it becomes a habit for him. Strategically set up the challenge again so that your teen faces something he already faced but is given an opportunity to accomplish it differently.

For example, in the picnic challenge, your teen planned a picnic for your family. You then went through the steps of the COPEC Method, beginning with Challenge, then Observe, then Process, and then Evaluate. Now it is time for Challenge Again and for your teen to make whatever changes he needs to make to complete the challenge successfully. It's up to him, not you, to figure out what needs to be changed in his efforts. There's no better way for your teen to fix his errors than to give him an opportunity to do the same challenge again.

Maybe he didn't pack the utensils the first time around. Maybe he didn't really think he was completely in charge of the picnic and expected you to take over. Of course you didn't do that, right? Good. Now is your chance to show him he is really trusted as a leader and give him an opportunity to lead again. Keep trying, and don't give up on your teen. Remember that failure is a struggle he must face in order to grow.

If you stepped in and took over for him in the middle of his challenge, being challenged again is a great opportunity for you to do things differently as well. Just because you are giving a challenge does not mean you are not facing your own challenge as well. Be honest with yourself and with your teen. If you messed up and stepped in when you shouldn't have, let him know you messed up. It shows honesty on your part and will help your teen be honest with you as well.

MORE CHALLENGES

Ideas for parents to
challenge their teens

Follow the COPEC method with each challenge you present to your teen.

IN THIS SECTION, we have compiled a few ideas for parents to challenge their teens with. Follow the COPEC method as closely as you can and give it a chance to work. Then come up with challenges of your own to present to your teen. Sharing these challenges with other parents is a great way to get ideas and insight about their successes and failures as well. Keep working at it.

It's Cleaning Time!

Challenge: Ask your teen to clean your house, apartment, or classroom completely.

This task may be something you think you have already done in the past. In fact, you might think that your teen already has chores to do and you do not need to do this task. *Do it anyway!* Since you have not done this before using the COPEC method, your results are more than likely going to be very different.

1. Challenge
Give your teen very clear instructions on what you want her to do in the challenge, but don't tell her how to do it.

If you want your house or classroom to be vacuumed, let your teen know that this is part of the cleaning you would like completed. If you expect all your things to be taken off shelves and dusted, windows cleaned, floors mopped, ceiling fans dusted, and so on, you must let her know very clearly that you want these things done.

It is not your responsibility to tell her to take notes. It is up to your teen whether she thinks she can remember what you are telling her. She may even expect you to give her a list. That is not your job! You may be thinking, "What if she fails or doesn't clean as I want it done?" This thought can easily run through your mind. It is important that *before* you give in and do the job you are asking your teen to do, *you must stop yourself*. Once you take over even the smallest part of the challenge you are asking her to do, she will expect you to take over other aspects as well.

2. Observe

Observe your teen during the challenge. Do not take over for her when things are not done the way you want them to be done, or the way you would do them yourself. Do not make faces or give your teen visual cues that might make her change the way she is doing things. Do not make noises of disapproval that will change her course of action. Simply let her be! This is your entire role in the Observe step of the COPEC method.

3. Process

Process this information with your teen. That means that you need to ask a lot of questions. What was the hardest part of completing this task? What was the easiest part? Did you understand exactly what I asked of you? Then you need to listen to her answers—really listen!

4. Evaluate

Evaluate her efforts. Do not evaluate her results. You are not trying to see how well she cleaned the house; instead, evaluate her
attempts at cleaning the house. This is not a way to give your teen
a participation trophy; on the contrary, she needs to know if she
failed. She also needs to know why she failed, and your job in this
step is, again, to ask questions to help her realize how to avoid the
same failure in the future. It is not your job to tell her why she
failed; instead, ask her questions to get her to come to her own
conclusions. Offer advice, if she says she is willing to hear it. This
opens dialogue and is the beginning of understanding, which
leads to a more effective relationship between you and your teen.

5. Challenge again

Immediately give your teen another challenge along with another
opportunity to change her efforts that led to failure in the original
challenge.

Does this mean that she is definitely going to fail the first challenge? No. If you are confused about this part, please make sure you
are not basing her success or failure on the outcome of the task.
You are simply finding ways to strengthen your teen, not only by
showing her how to recognize her failures but also by encouraging
her in her successes.

No participation trophies! Only give her encouragement on her
actual successful efforts, as well as encouraging her to overcome
her failures. Don't be fake with your evaluation—no "Good job"
fluff, if a good job was not done.

So, for example, if she was supposed to clean a particular room
in your house but did not vacuum, you could—in the Challenge
Again step—say something like, "You did a good job cleaning
the windows and dusting. Thank you for that. You also forgot to

vacuum the carpet, and I know I mentioned wanting that done and that you said you understood what I asked. So go ahead and finish vacuuming the carpet please, and let me know when you are done so I can take a look at it with you. But again, great job on the windows and the dusting."

This is the type of communication you are striving for. It is honest, it is not filled with fluff, and more importantly, it encourages your teen to persevere and not give up.

Plant a Garden

Challenge. Ask your teen to plant a garden in your backyard.

We love this challenge. Planting a garden offers a great opportunity for your teen to see hard work and continuous effort pay off. Challenge your teen to plant a garden with some sort of fruit or vegetable plant. Growing something of sustenance helps your teen to see the *fruits* of his labor! Follow the steps and make sure you let him do it on his own.

Get a Weekend Job

Challenge. Ask your teen to find a way to earn money on weekends.

One of the best ways for your teen to gain a sense of responsibility is to earn money. It does not have to be a full-time job with a 401(k) and vacation pay, but something that helps your teen gain respect for hard work. If you have a lawn mower, challenge him to start up a lawn mowing service for your neighbors—but he has to do this on his own! Don't have a lawn mower? What about a pet-walking service? There are thousands of ways for your teen to make some spending money on the weekends with very little time involvement. But leave it up to him. Let him go and find a way to make this happen on his own.

More Ideas

Follow all COPEC Method steps for all these Challenge ideas. Then come up with some of your own to challenge your teen with.

- ▶ Do the laundry—including folding and putting clothes away.
- ▶ Set and clear the table.
- ▶ Wash and put away the dishes.
- ▶ Feed and walk the family pets; clean birdcages and litter boxes.
- ▶ Prepare his own lunches for school.
- ▶ Cook dinner one night a week.
- ▶ Do yardwork.
- ▶ Wash the family car.

CLOSING THOUGHTS

THROUGHOUT THIS BOOK you have practiced the COPEC method and learned how to challenge your teen to help him become a leader. Although you may be doing everything right and following every step of the COPEC method, you may be having a hard time and struggling to see a difference in your teen at first. As Jesus says: Fear not!

You are not alone, and you are not necessarily doing something wrong. Using the COPEC method takes time and repetition. So if you don't have it down completely, be patient and persistent. This advice probably sounds similar to the advice you give your teen.

Letting your teen know you are working on a challenge yourself, while sharing your successes and failures, can be a great way to build a deeper relationship. If you fail during your training, it is okay and even beneficial to let your teen know that you failed, but more importantly, that you refused to give up. What a great example you will set for your teen this way!

ABOUT THE AUTHORS

ALAN MIGLIORATO is the author of *The Manly Art of Raising a Daughter*. He has appeared on EWTN's *At Home with Jim and Joy* television show as well as numerous radio shows throughout the country. He is the founder of Adventure Catholic Formation Leadership Training and has a certification in youth ministry from the University of Dayton, as well as being a veteran of the U.S. Army. Alan has been married to the same wonderful woman since 1993, has raised three beautiful daughters, and is the owner of a sign and advertising company in the Orlando area. His passions are spending time with his family and leading others to know Jesus.

DARRYL DZIEDZIC has been involved in professional youth ministry for more than seventeen years. He is a seminary graduate and has a bachelor's degree in philosophy and a master's degree in theology. The father of two incredible boys, Darryl seeks to help teens become the type of leader God intends them to be by focusing on God.

Both Darryl and Alan offer parish missions, youth missions, speaking engagements, parent and teen retreat weekends, ongoing formation training for parents, and interactive weekend experiences for parents and high-school-age teens. You can see more of their work at www.adventurecatholic.com.

Sophia Institute

Sophia Institute is a nonprofit institution that seeks to nurture the spiritual, moral, and cultural life of souls and to spread the Gospel of Christ in conformity with the authentic teachings of the Roman Catholic Church.

Sophia Institute Press fulfills this mission by offering translations, reprints, and new publications that afford readers a rich source of the enduring wisdom of mankind.

Sophia Institute also operates the popular online resource CatholicExchange.com. *Catholic Exchange* provides world news from a Catholic perspective as well as daily devotionals and articles that will help readers to grow in holiness and live a life consistent with the teachings of the Church.

In 2013, Sophia Institute launched Sophia Institute for Teachers to renew and rebuild Catholic culture through service to Catholic education. With the goal of nurturing the spiritual, moral, and cultural life of souls, and an abiding respect for the role and work of teachers, we strive to provide materials and programs that are at once enlightening to the mind and ennobling to the heart; faithful and complete, as well as useful and practical.

Sophia Institute gratefully recognizes the Solidarity Association for preserving and encouraging the growth of our apostolate over the course of many years. Without their generous and timely support, this book would not be in your hands.

www.SophiaInstitute.com
www.CatholicExchange.com
www.SophiaInstituteforTeachers.org

Sophia Institute Press® is a registered trademark of Sophia Institute.
Sophia Institute is a tax-exempt institution as defined by the
Internal Revenue Code, Section 501(c)(3). Tax ID 22-2548708.